A Special Gift for

Mom

from

Savannah

on

August 15, 2003

Date

Visit Tyndale's exciting Web site at www.tyndale.com

Love Notes from God for Busy Moms

By Helen M. Young. Copyright © 2003 by Mary Hollingsworth , Shady Oaks Studio, 1507 Shirley Way, Bedford, Texas 76022. All rights reserved.

Artwork copyright © 2000 Artville, LLC.

Published by Tyndale House Publishers, Inc.

Research and writing associate: Vicki P. Graham

Series General Editor: Mary Hollingsworth

Published in Association with Educational Publishing Concepts, Wheaton, IL.

ISBN 0-8423-7754-9

Printed in Canada

02 03 04 05 06 07 — 6 5 4 3 2 1

Mary Hollingsworth's

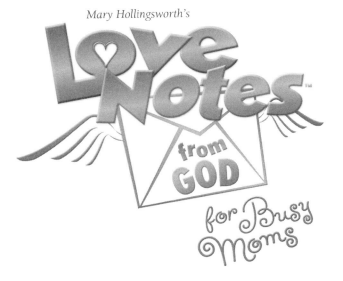

Mary Hollingsworth's

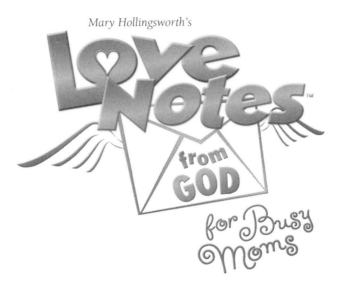

Love Notes from GOD for Busy Moms

by
Helen M. Young

Foreword by
Mary Hollingsworth

Contents

Foreword

Sitting on Helen Young's deck, looking down the Malibu hills past her precious Pepperdine University campus to the placid and glistening Pacific Ocean, I feel the serene presence of the beautiful woman in whose home and friendship I reside.

Helen is a second mother to me. And she's not a mother just to me, but to her own four wonderful children, to her grandchildren who call her "Honey," to literally thousands of present and former university students, and to a myriad of people around the world who have loved and admired her through the years. She's the matriarch of Pepperdine where she was a professor and her beloved husband, M. Norvel Young, was president, chancellor, and chancellor emeritus for several decades.

Like my own mother, Helen exhibits the Christian qualities mothers everywhere should pursue—warmth, nurturing, hospitality, genuineness, deep and abiding love, godliness, intelligence, hope, faith, optimism, joy, and strength.

At this writing Helen is not here. Approaching her eighty-third birthday, she asked me to house-sit while she traveled to Albania to teach the Bible to the lost and lonely people there for several weeks. I was not surprised. That's just who she is. It's her nature to mother and teach children everywhere, whether her own or some of God's other children.

This book of love notes is for busy moms from one of the buisiest and greatest mothers of our time. You will be blessed so richly by it. Enjoy!

Mary Hollingsworth

Series General Editor

As a mother loves
and comforts her
child, so I will love and
comfort you.

—Isaiah 66:13, adapted

*N*othing is
impossible with God.

———————

—Luke 1:37

CHAPTER ONE

The Note

You Are Loved

The hospital was unusually quiet that bleak winter evening, quiet and still. Nurse June Black stood in the doorway of her new ICU patient who had suffered a heart attack just hours earlier.

"How are you feeling, Bernice?" she asked the woman in the bed, who had steadfastly refused to give out any information about herself. "Could I call someone to let them know where you are?"

"No, no, I'm alone," Bernice's voice quavered. "Well, I have a mother, but we haven't spoken in years. Would you . . . ?" and she broke off.

"Now, Bernice, let me help you," June said, sensing her patient needed to say more.

"Then would you get me a piece of paper and a pencil?" she asked.

When the nurse returned with pad and pencil in hand, she helped Bernice adjust her oxygen mask and IV tubes so she could write. June noted that Bernice's heart and breathing rates increased as she deliberated over the writing pad, and June's nursing instincts quickened as she wondered how a woman only forty years old could exhibit such dangerous symptoms.

"I'll be OK—don't worry," Bernice told her, and bent over her work. "I promise to buzz if I need something."

June discreetly left Bernice to her privacy and went to the nurses' station, where she once again checked the records to see if any kind of relative or friend might have been listed. It seemed as if only minutes passed before the monitors for Bernice began to beep. June hurried to the room to find her patient crying and wheezing.

"Please, I'm scared," Bernice whispered, trying to hide her tears. "I don't feel right; something's wrong."

"You're young; you'll recover," June assured her.

"I think it's time to call my mother. I'll never

forgive myself if I don't. Will you do it?" she asked.

Nodding her assent, June quickly took the information from Bernice and promised she'd call immediately. Then, after reassuring the anxious woman, June hurried to her station and dialed the number.

On her first try she was rewarded with the voice of a woman who identified herself as the mother of Bernice.

When June began to inform the mother of her daughter's condition, the mother spurted in near-hysteria: "She's not dying, is she? Oh, God, don't let her die. Where is she?"

June tried to explain Bernice's condition, but the woman continued to insist the doctors not let her daughter die. Huge sobs echoed through the phone as the despairing mother said she'd get to the hospital as soon as possible.

"Please help her hang on," she gulped through tears.

June again tried to tell Bernice's mother that the best possible care was being given.

"You don't understand," the mother cried. "Ten years ago my daughter left her husband and ran away with what I thought was a cult group. She came to me to try to explain why, and I told her she had embarrassed me, and that I never wanted to see her again.

"I told her I hated her," she whispered. "I have to tell her I love her. I have to ask her forgiveness. I can't live without her forgiveness."

Ending the conversation with the distraught mother, June hurried to tell Bernice of the phone call. Before she could enter the room, the monitors sounded their alarms. Bernice was in cardiac arrest. Doctors and staff swarmed down the hall with their emergency equipment and swiftly began resuscitation on the unmoving patient.

"God, please don't let her die. Let her and her mother resolve this fight," June prayed. "Let them find love."

Despite all efforts, Bernice did not respond. The doctors pronounced her dead and sadly gathered their equipment and left the room. June sank to the bed beside the still body and tried to think what she would tell the mother. She decided to ask the nurses to leave Bernice in her room for a couple of hours to see if the mother would arrive and, perhaps, help with arrangements.

Too soon, June saw an elderly but energetic lady walking down the ICU corridor toward the nurses' station. June intercepted her and said, "You must be Bernice's mother," and gently guided her to a sitting area.

The hurt and pain that reflected from the older woman's face as June told her the sad news caused June to shed tears, too, in silent compassion.

"I'm so sorry," June said as she held the woman. "So very sorry."

"I never hated her, you know. I loved her," she said. Then, looking up at June, "I want to see her. I have to say good-bye."

June led her to Bernice's room. Silently, she prayed, *God, give this woman your peace. Show her she's loved.*

While the grieving mother stood at her daughter's bedside, June tried not to look at the sad good-bye. She busied herself straightening the area around Bernice's bed. Suddenly her eyes fell on the notepad she had taken to Bernice earlier in the evening. June didn't think her weak patient had been able to write anything, but there it was in plain, trembling black letters.

June was openly crying now as she put the tablet into the mother's hands. She watched as the mother read the note once, then twice. Her tormented face grew peaceful. Her eyes began to shine through their wetness.

"Thank you, God," the mother whispered as she kissed her daughter, handed the note to June, and left the room.

June wiped her eyes so she too could read:

My Dearest Mom,

I forgive you. I hope and pray you will also forgive me. I know that you love me. I love you too.

Bernice

The heart of a mother
is a deep abyss
at the bottom of which
you will always discover
forgiveness.

—Honoré de Balzac

Fear Not

As a small child John was quite frightened of storms, which often came in the middle of the night in New Guinea where his parents were missionaries. It surely didn't help that they had no electricity.

In the darkness, John would cry out, "Mom! Mom, hurry! I'm scared."

Immediately his mother would come and wrap her loving arms around him in the darkness. She reminded him of how God was keeping him safe. Night after night John continued in his fear of storms.

Finally, one thunder-filled night, as John shook with fear, his mother repeated, "It's all right, God is here with you."

John replied with a whimper, even as he clung more tightly to his mother, "I know God is with me, but sometimes I just need God with skin on."

A Love Note from God

I am your rock, your fortress,
your place of safety.
Run to me for protection,
and I will save you, because
I love you.

—Psalm 18:2, adapted

Your Love Note to God

Dear God,

_____

_____

_____

_____

_____

_____

_____

_____

I love you. _____

$\mathcal{G}$od pardons like a mother,
who kisses the offense
into everlasting
forgetfulness.

—Author Unknown

$\mathcal{B}$ecause you refresh
other people,
I love you, and I will
also refresh you.

———

—Proverbs 11:25, adapted

CHAPTER TWO

The White Gardenia

You Are Extraordinary

*E*very year on my birthday, from the time I turned twelve, one white gardenia was delivered anonymously to me at my house. There was never a card or note, and calls to the florist were in vain because the purchase was always made in cash.

After a while, I stopped trying to discover the identity of the sender. I just delighted in the beauty and heady perfume of that one magical, perfect white flower nestled in folds of soft pink tissue paper.

But I never stopped imagining who the sender might be. Some of my happiest moments were

spent in daydreams about someone wonderful
and exciting, but too shy or eccentric to make
known his or her identity. In my teen years, it
was fun to speculate that the sender might be a
boy I had a crush on, or even someone I didn't
know who had noticed me.

My mother often contributed to my specula-
tions. She'd ask me if there was someone for
whom I had done a special kindness, who might
be showing appreciation anonymously. She
reminded me of the times when I'd been riding
my bike, and our neighbor drove up with her car
full of groceries and children. I always helped her
unload the car and made sure the children didn't
run into the road. Or maybe the mystery sender
was the old man across the street. I often retrieved
his mail during the winter, so he wouldn't have to
venture down his icy steps.

My mother did her best to foster my imagina-
tion about the gardenia. She wanted her children

to be creative. She also wanted us to feel cherished and loved, not just by her, but by the world at large.

When I was seventeen, a boy broke my heart. The night he called for the last time, I cried myself to sleep. When I awoke in the morning, there was a message scribbled on my mirror in red lipstick: "Heartily know, when half-gods go, the gods arrive." I thought about that quotation from Emerson for a long time, and I left it where my mother had written it until my heart healed. When I finally went for the glass cleaner, my mother knew that everything was all right again.

But there were some hurts my mother couldn't heal. A month before my high school graduation, my father died suddenly of a heart attack. My feelings ranged from simple grief to abandonment, fear, distrust, and overwhelming anger that my dad was missing some of the most important events in my life. I became completely uninterested in my upcoming graduation, the senior-class play, and the prom events that I had worked on and looked forward to. I even considered staying home to attend college instead of going away as I had planned, because it felt safer.

My mother, in the midst of her own grief, wouldn't hear of me missing out on any of these things. The day before my father died, she and I had gone shopping for a prom dress and had found a spectacular one—yards and yards of dotted Swiss in red, white, and blue. Wearing it made me feel like Scarlett O'Hara. But it was the wrong size, and when my father died the next day, I forgot all about the dress.

My mother didn't. The day before the prom, I found that dress waiting for me—in the right size. It was draped majestically over the living room sofa, presented to me artistically and lovingly. I may not have cared about having a new dress, but my mother did.

She cared how we children felt about ourselves. She imbued us with a sense of the magic in the world, and she gave us the ability to see beauty, even in the face of adversity.

In truth, my mother wanted her children to see themselves much like the gardenia: lovely, strong, perfect, with an aura of magic and, perhaps, a bit of mystery.

My mother died when I was twenty-two, only ten days after I was married. That was the year the gardenias stopped coming.

—Marsha Arons

A mom's gift is always the best, because it's wrapped in gentle love and tied up with tender heartstrings.

—Mary Hollingsworth

The Inner Woman

Two eighteen-year-old secretaries were taking a coffee break, sunning themselves outside the photographer's studio where they worked. A rather homely, middle-aged woman came out of the studio. One of the girls, looking up from filing her nails, glanced at her and commented acidly to her friend, "Frankly, if I had her face, I wouldn't dare to have my picture taken."

Later on, back at work, the two secretaries were stunned to hear one photographer say to another, "You remember that woman in her fifties who was in here twenty minutes ago? I like to photograph that kind of face—a face with real character in it. There was a certain patient steadfastness in her eyes. The strong lines around her mouth showed determination.

"You know," he concluded, "pretty faces are a dime a dozen. Time and pain and cares have not touched them yet. But that woman's lined face— that reflected some powerful qualities inside of her. She's a mother."

A Love Note from Heaven

Did you know your beauty
comes from inside you?
I love your gentle and quiet spirit.
You are worth so much to me.

—1 Peter 3:4, adapted

Your Love Note to God

Dear God,

_____

_____

_____

_____

_____

_____

_____

_____

I love you. _____

Nothing else will ever make
you as happy or as sad,
as proud or as tired,
as motherhood.

—Elia Parsons

I had your mother give
birth to you.
I caused you to trust me
from the time you
were a baby.
So lean on me now
when trouble is near.
I won't be far away
and I will help you.

———

—Psalm 22:9–11, adapted

CHAPTER THREE

Mommy, Your Mommy Wants to See You

You Are Needed

$\mathcal{B}$ecause my father was an alcoholic, my sister and brother and I clung to our mother while we were growing up. When mother was suddenly killed in a car accident at age forty-nine, we were completely unprepared and deeply shaken. My youngest sister, Karen, was only fourteen and was too afraid to go and live with my father, so she came to live with me in Nebraska.

Karen and I shared good times and bad in the next eight years and always talked about why God had taken away our mother—the only stable thing in our lives—when we were so young and so dependent on her.

When I married a wheat farmer and moved to western Nebraska, we had a daughter and son, Shannon and Jay.

On the farm, harvest season was an especially difficult time because we needed so much extra help, and I couldn't call on my mom and dad as so many neighbors did. Other than my husband's parents, neither of us had any extended family available to assist us during the harvest. When other farmers would talk about their families, my heart would ache for my mother. I wondered if somehow she knew how I was, that I was married and had children, that I missed her so terribly.

One busy day, when I had taken a break under the shade trees, I told God that I knew he was busy too with so many things in the world, but that if it wasn't too much trouble, could he please send some sort of sign that my mother knew where I was and hadn't forgotten me.

I needed just a little something to feel her presence.

A few days later I was giving Jay a bottle when three-year-old Shannon came in from the front yard where she had been swinging. She had a serious look on her face. Very deliberately she said, "Mommy, your mommy wants to see you."

I said, "What?"

Again she said very intently, "Your mommy wants to see you."

I was stunned! I looked at her in disbelief as she continued, "Hurry, Mommy, she's waiting!"

I got up with Jay in my arms, and as we were going out the door I said, "Where is she?"

"She's here!" Shannon replied. "I'll show you."

We walked over to the swing set and Shannon pointed above it and said, "There, right there!"

I tried to be calm and act nonchalant as I asked, "Where is she now?"

Shannon pointed to the space right beside me and said, "Right there."

I was shaken to the core, so stunned I could hardly speak. I wanted so badly to feel her, to talk to her, but in the end all I could utter was a simple, "Mom, I love you!"

I suppose that's all that really needed to be said. She was there with me. She knew about my life. She was a friend to my children. She already knew the feelings of my heart. I was sure of it!

This incredible experience lasted about fifteen minutes. Shannon was extremely calm and unaffected throughout. This event was nothing unusual to her, I realized. When I finally asked Shannon if my mother was still there, she replied, "She's gone now."

Before this, I had never discussed my mother

45

with Shannon, nor was she even aware that she ought to have another grandma. Shannon never again brought up what happened that day, but I was completely awed and humbled by this very loving, undeniable answer to my simple prayer. Whenever I think about it, a sense of peace envelops me like a warm blanket. I feel great joy knowing that my Father in heaven cares about me enough to so vividly show his love.

—Kristin Peterson Linton

Mothers have amazing vision. They prepare their children for a future they cannot see.

Fear Not

After a fire in Yellowstone National Forest, rangers began their trek up a mountain to assess the inferno's damage.

One ranger found a bird literally petrified in ashes, perched statuesquely on the ground at the base of a tree.

Somewhat sickened by the eerie sight, he tipped over the bird with a stick.

When he gently struck it, three tiny chicks scurried from under their dead mother's wings. The loving mother, keenly aware of impending disaster, had carried her offspring to the base of

47

the tree and gathered them under her wings, instinctively knowing that the toxic smoke would rise. She could have flown to safety but had refused to abandon her babies. When the blaze had arrived and the heat had scorched her small body, the mother remained steadfast.

Because she had been willing to die, those under the cover of her wings would live.

—Retold from facts in the public record.

A Love Note from God

I will cover you
with my feathers,
and under my wings
you will find refuge.

—Psalm 91:4, adapted

Your Love Note to God

Dear God,

_____

_____

_____

_____

_____

_____

_____

_____

I love you. _____

Whenever I want to feel especially
good about myself,
I just remember that I have
you for a mom.

—Mary Hollingsworth

I will make everything
possible for you if
you believe.

—Mark 9:23, adapted

CHAPTER FOUR

No Greater Love

You Are Giving

*A*cry in the night from my two-year-old daughter jolted me awake for the third night in a row. As I entered her room, Marissa was sitting on her bed, holding her head and crying. Between sobs she repeatedly told me that her head was "ouchie."

Her complaining increased and I called the doctor. After a series of tests, the doctor sat my husband and me down to explain the problem. David and I clasped each other as the doctor told us Marissa had the symptoms of a brain tumor; he needed to do a brain scan and MRI, to literally peek inside her brain.

We were devastated. I immediately called Marissa's grandmother, Barb. "Stepmother" never seemed to convey the special relationship that Barb and I shared. I was only fourteen when my mother passed away. (Looking back, I'm impressed at how my father raised three teenage girls alone before marrying Barb.) So Barb became my special mom to do things with, to help plan my wedding, rush to the hospital when I gave birth, and love my children as her own grandchildren.

During this difficult time with Marissa, Barb did much to encourage and support me, even though she was dealing with her own bad headache from a sinus infection. One day she came rushing to my side when I found myself sobbing from all the pressures of Marissa's impending tests, caring for two kids, and pregnancy.

The possibility of a brain tumor was unthinkable to Barb. Marissa had not lived yet, she told me. She said she prayed that if someone should have a tumor, it should be her, not Marissa. She had lived a full life of love, marriage, children, and grandchildren.

The next week, my father and Barb sat with David and me as Marissa underwent the MRI. It would be twenty-four hours before the doctors could give us any results. The next morning the doctor told us that the MRI did not show a brain tumor or anything else serious. The MRI did, however, show that Marissa had a severe sinus infection. At her age that would account for the headaches and the dizziness.

After a round of antibiotics, Marissa was back to normal, and so was family life. Our third child arrived in March, and then we met for our annual gathering at Dad and Barb's house. Barb was carefree, but Dad seemed very tense. Something did not seem right.

Later my sisters and I agreed that something was wrong. The following Monday Dad asked if we had noticed anything different about Barb. She was not acting normal, he said, and she made foolish mistakes or shopped excessively. She was also complaining of a constant throbbing headache.

The next week, things escalated. After an office exam, the doctor sent Barb immediately to the hospital for further testing. I remember sitting with Barb as the neurologist gave her a simple test. What day was it? Who was president? Why was she here? Somehow I found the strength not to cry in front of Barb when I saw that she couldn't pass the test.

I knew in my heart that something was terribly wrong. I wanted to run away and hide and cry as I had done when my mother had died.

The next day, after an MRI, the doctors made the diagnosis: Barb had a massive brain tumor. The doctors thought it started growing last winter when her "sinus headaches" began. By now it was very large and surgery was a must.

Barb never made it to surgery. The tumor hemorrhaged, and she died less than one week after being diagnosed with it.

Were the similarities in conditions and timing between Barb and Marissa a mere coincidence? Or are there a handful of souls on earth who love so much that they would literally give up their lives for someone they loved? I am so grateful for the rare opportunity to have been loved so deeply by two mothers. My new challenge is to remember their examples of strength and love as I wipe away my own daughters' tears.

—Jill Reed

A grandmother is a mother
who has a second chance.

—Anonymous

Why Mothers Get Gray

A few months ago, I was making several phone calls in the family room where my three-year-old daughter was playing quietly with her five-month-old brother, Nathan. Nathan loves Adrianne, who has been learning how to mother him gently since he was born.

I suddenly realized that the children were no longer in view. Panic-stricken, I quickly hung up the phone and went looking. Down the hall, and around the corner, I found Adrianne and her baby brother playing cheerfully on the floor of the nursery.

Relieved and upset, I shouted, "Adrianne, you know you are not allowed to carry Nathan! He is too little and you'll hurt him if you drop him!"

Startled, she answered, "I didn't, Mommy."

Knowing the baby couldn't crawl, I suspiciously demanded, "Well, then, how did he get all the way into the nursery?"

Confident of my approval for her obedience, she said with a smile, "I rolled him!"

—Author unknown

A Love Note from God

I will take care of you.
I will give you everything to enjoy.
Be happy and be ready to share.

—1 Timothy 6:17—19, adapted

Your Love Note to God

Dear God,

_____

_____

_____

_____

_____

_____

_____

_____

I love you. _____

Mothers like you are
God's love in action.

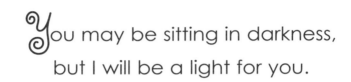
You may be sitting in darkness,
but I will be a light for you.

—Micah 7:8, adapted

CHAPTER FIVE

The Sacrifice

You Are Remembered

*L*ydia was two years old when she emigrated from Ireland to the United States with her mother's friends. World War II had been over for two years, and Lydia's mother simply could not continue to support three daughters any longer. Their father had been killed in action near the end of the war, and she was left as breadwinner and single parent.

The only recourse was to let her friends adopt Lydia and take her to the States with them where she'd be assured of a comfortable lifestyle and loving parents.

Lydia lived a fairy-tale family life based on a

strong Christian upbringing, and she was taught about her birth mother's loving sacrifice of letting her be adopted. However, in a few years Lydia's adoptive parents lost contact with her mother and sisters, and by the time she graduated from high school, all she remembered was the story of coming to America and her mother's maiden name of Sweeny.

By the time Lydia turned fifty, she had lost both her adoptive parents and her husband. They were never able to have children, and now Lydia was acutely aware of impending loneliness as she aged. For some reason she felt herself drawn to thoughts of Ireland, and she wondered if God had a mission for her back in her homeland.

Lydia decided since she had plenty of money, no family, and no real ties to anything, that she should visit the home of her ancestors. Specifically, she yearned to feel a sense of family somewhere, a sense of belonging.

Ireland proved to be as beautiful and friendly as she could have hoped. She indeed felt a belonging.

One day, during a visit to a tiny coastal village, she sat on the dock pondering her feelings.

"God, am I here for a reason?" she prayed. "Show me clearly why."

Lydia had no sooner said "amen" than she heard cheerful voices from a couple of women about her age.

"Oh, hello, Colleen." They each greeted her as they passed on by.

"Wait, I'm not Colleen," she called out to them.

"Well, now, sure you are," one woman said. "Don't be fooling us." And she turned to peer closely at Lydia. "Why, *begorra*, you're not Colleen!"

"Is so," said the other woman, and she stepped

up to see. "A twin then you are. Tell me now, you are related to our friend Colleen, yes?"

As Lydia explained that she was an American tourist but was born near this village before moving to America, the women became incredulous.

"Say, now," one said, "do you know your mother's maiden name?"

When Lydia replied "Sweeny," their mouths dropped open. Then they sat on the dock with Lydia and told her their story.

It was almost a legend in the village about the brave and loving Sweeny woman who had given up her youngest daughter in order to provide for her other two and save the wee one, too. The mother had been in contact with Lydia's family for several years before she moved back to her hometown to be near her parents. In that village, whatever last name you were born with proved to be the name you'd carry forever, despite marriages or deaths or divorces. So that was the reason Lydia could not locate her mother or sisters when she tried so many years ago.

"But the good news is," one of the women said, pulling Lydia to her feet with a swift hug, "you have an entire family right here! The reason we called you Colleen is because you look exactly like our friend whose mother made that amazing sacrifice. And she has a sister, she does, who favors you, too. They both have husbands and families here as well."

"But the very best thing is," said the other woman as she beamed at Lydia, "your mother is here, alive and healthy as can be, she is. She has told all of us that she knew that someday she'd be seeing her beautiful daughter again, that somehow the Lord would provide, and so he has—he has."

Sometime during the jubilant homecoming that ensued when the women escorted Lydia to her mother's house and gathered up her sisters, she found a moment alone to raise her tear-filled eyes to heaven and whisper, "Thank you, God, for giving me back my mother."

—Vicki Graham

Being a good mom
isn't complicated.
Only one thing is needed.
When you, yourself,
dine on the presence of God,
your children will find in you
what they need.

—Elisa Morgan

A Judge's Wisdom

Many centuries ago in a country in the Middle East, a young judge wanted more than anything to be wise. He prayed nightly for God to help him be fair and just.

"God," he prayed one evening, "please show me I'm learning to be wise so I won't worry about it so much. Send me a case where I can feel your guidance."

Shortly thereafter, two women appeared in his court.

"Sir," one of them began, "we live in the same house, just the two of us, and recently I had a baby. When it was three days old, this woman's baby was born, too. But her baby died in the night when she rolled over it in her sleep and smothered it.

"Then she got up in the night and took my son from me while I was asleep, laid her dead child in my arms, and took mine to sleep beside her. In the morning when I tried to feed my baby, it was dead! But when it came light outside, I saw that it wasn't my son at all."

Then the other woman interrupted, "It certainly was her son, and the living child is mine."

"No," the first woman said, "the dead one is yours, and the live one is mine." And so they argued back and forth before the judge.

"OK, let's get the facts straight," he said. "Both of you claim the living child, and each says that the dead child belongs to the other. All right, let me think on this."

The judge spent the entire time on his knees, locked in his chambers. "God, I asked for a sign, but it has to be your wisdom in this case, not mine!"

Suddenly the judge stopped praying and started laughing. "God, you are so awesome," he said. "I see that to be wise I should always ask you for your wisdom. Thanks, Lord."

73

The judge reentered the courtroom with confidence. "Here's what we're going to do, ladies. I have asked the officers to bring in a sword." The judge turned to his men and ordered, "Divide the living child in two and give half to each of these women!"

The woman who really was the mother of the child, and who loved him very much, cried out, "Oh, no, sir! Give her the child—don't kill him!"

But the other woman said, "All right, it will be neither yours nor mine; divide it between us!"

Then the judge said, "Give the baby to the woman who wants him to live, for she is the mother!"

Word of the judge's decision spread quickly throughout the country, and all the people respected and revered him for his great wisdom. But the young judge never forgot how God used him to deliver a wise lesson to two young mothers.

—Adapted from 1 Kings 3:16–28

A Love Note from God

I am the God of all comfort.
I will comfort you
every time you have trouble
so that you will be able
to comfort others.

—2 Corinthians 1:4, adapted

Your Love Note to God

Dear God,

_____

_____

_____

_____

_____

_____

_____

_____

I love you. _____

$\mathcal{D}$on't be afraid!

When you have troubles

I am with you.

You are very important to me.

—Isaiah 43:1-4, adapted

$\mathcal{D}$epend on me in whatever you do, and your plans will succeed.

—Proverbs 16:3, adapted

CHAPTER SIX

Watching with Love

You Are Protected

*A*s a boy growing up in the city it was somewhat dangerous for me to walk to school all by myself. So my mother paid Harriet, a neighborhood girl a few years older than I, to be responsible for getting me to and from school each day. Harriet was paid five cents a day for this service.

As I grew older, I became very conscious of what I believed was an enormous amount of money going into Harriet's hands. So I went to my mother and told her that there was no need for her to pay Harriet any longer, that she should give me the nickel each day, and I would walk myself to school. I assured her that I could do it with no problem at all. At first my mother resisted the idea, but I kept on begging and begging until she finally gave in.

She sighed and said, "OK, if you're very careful, I'll give you the nickel a day, and you can put the money in the bank and save it to buy Christmas presents for your sisters."

That seemed like a good idea. So from that time on I walked myself to school, collected the money, and did not allow my mom's nickels to leave the household. This went on for several years.

Years later, when my mother had passed on, I was at a family get-together with my sisters, and I reminded them of my independent spirit, even when I was a child. I proudly reminded them of how I had walked myself to school, and how I had needed no one's help in getting there and back each day, and how that translated into good presents for them at Christmastime.

My sisters laughed at me uncontrollably. Finally, one of them caught her breath enough to say, "Did you think that you went to school alone and came home alone?"

"Well, yes," I said. "Didn't I?"

"Every day when you left the house, Mom followed you. And when you came out of school at the end of the day, she was there. She always made sure that you didn't notice her, but she watched over you coming and going, just to make sure you were safe and that nobody hurt you."

"No, it can't be," I protested.

"Didn't it ever occur to you that there was something strange about the fact that when you knocked on the door she didn't answer right away?" my sister asked.

"I never really thought about it," I said.

"That's because she would follow you home,

then sneak in the back door. When she opened the front door and let you in, you were always left with the impression that you had been on your own, when in reality she had been watching over you all the time."

The Lord watches over you always. He never gets tired and never sleeps.

—Psalm 121:4, adapted

When the Wind Blows

Six-year-old Dana and four-year-old Kelly screamed as the tornado howled through their house. Their mother, Pam, held them so tightly she thought her fingers would be squeezed off. Just five minutes earlier the two children had been playing on the living room floor with Dana's new stuffed toy—Barney, the purple dinosaur—which she still clutched as they ran for safety in the storm cellar.

As the wind's suction threatened to tear the children from Pam's arms, Dana's precious purple friend went flying. She screamed hysterically. Her mother couldn't tell if it was from fear or the loss of her beloved Barney.

It doesn't really matter, Pam thought, as she realized they weren't going to make it to the cellar. *We're going to be blown away, anyway. God, please don't let my babies be hurt.*

Desperate now, she pushed the babies into a ditch and laid across them as she watched her house literally be blown into splinters. Amazingly, Pam and the children weren't hurt. Their worst wound was the terror they had just survived.

In the eerie quiet that followed the storm, Pam surveyed the destruction. She again was reminded that the house and furnishings looked as if they had been through a shredder. The quiet was broken only by the sobbing of Dana.

"Mommy, I'm so scared," she whimpered. "Doesn't God love us any more?"

Pam's heart was broken. "God, I know you didn't send a storm to destroy our home, but Dana is too young to understand," she prayed. "Can you show this little child that you still love her?"

Her prayer was interrupted by a shout from Dana, "Mommy, look in the tree!"

"Incredible, God. Marvelous. Awesome." Pam couldn't think of enough words to describe what she saw. For there, perched in a fork of a tree, sat the smiling purple dinosaur, with not a rip, not a tear, not a sign of having flown out of the house and through the branches.

"See, Mommy," Dana tugged Pam's hand as she gazed in rapture at her toy. "God saved Barney. That means he'll save what you love most, too."

Pam gathered both her babies into her arms. "He already has, Dana, he already has."

A Love Note from God

I am with you
every place you go.
I will gently put my hand on you.
My strong right hand will hold
you and lead you.

—Psalm 139:7-10, adapted

Your Love Note to God

Dear God,

_____

_____

_____

_____

_____

_____

_____

I love you, _____

$\mathcal{B}$e humble and I will lift you up
when the right time comes.
Give all your worries to me,
because I care about you.

—1 Peter 5:6–7, adapted.

*D*epend on me in
whatever you do, and
your plans will succeed.

———————————

—Proverbs 16:3, adapted

CHAPTER SEVEN

The Sweetest Sound on Earth

You Are Honored

$\mathcal{N}$ ora arrived late for church that Mother's Day morning. It was a deliberate move for this great-grandmother who had attended services at the same church for most of her eighty years and rarely was late or absent.

This morning was different. Nora did not want to face the congregation on this Mother's Day without the presence of any of her three generations of children.

Usually Nora took pride that most of the seats around her were vacant and that, even after her husband died, she was courageous enough to continue occupying their traditional pew. Today the empty seats only reminded her of how empty her heart was.

"Four generations and none to show off but me," she mused as she surveyed the pews packed with proud relatives and children. Sure, Nora had beautiful flower arrangements and loving Mother's Day cards at the house. And she had carefully pinned to her jacket a fragrant gardenia, a traditional gift from her oldest for dozens of years.

By her corsage at least her peers would know she wasn't forgotten, thought Nora as she recalled that, for this church, Mother's Day was the day for showing off children, grandchildren, and, in her case, great-grandchildren. Saddened by memories of pews being filled with her own family, Nora diverted her mind with fond memories of the babies coming to church with her.

Startled out of her reverie, Nora heard the young people seated at the front of the church singing softly to indicate worship was beginning.

God, help me, she thought. *I'm so embarrassed to be here alone, and I'm so afraid I'll cry. You know I'm too proud to do that in public.*

The young singers' voices grew louder: "When peace like a river . . ." The words wafted across the sanctuary.

"It is well with my soul," my foot, Nora thought. *I'm alone and they sing the very song we sang at Bill's graveside. Lord, I don't want to have a pity party. Don't you love me?*

Though she would never admit it to her church friends, Nora knew she heard a voice inside her say, "Look around you and see how much I love you."

Startled to the depths of her soul, Nora did as she was told. At first all she saw across the auditorium were the families and hordes of little children, it seemed. Then her eyes misted over as she realized what God was showing her.

Oh God, I see it, I see it, her mind raced. *There's Mrs. Plumley, recently widowed and not a relative within a thousand miles. There's Twila who could never have children and Sheila whose boys were killed in that horrible car wreck. And there's Sister Pearl. Her mind's too far gone to even realize her kids are sitting right beside her.*

Nora's eyes ranged across the congregation, and as the chorus swelled to the final strains of "It Is Well with My Soul," she bowed her head in quiet prayer: "Father, forgive me for being selfish and proud. You've shown me how blessed I am to have such a healthy, happy family, and they all love each other so much. I will take joy in what you've given me. Thank you for reminding me how much you love me."

It was then Nora heard the sweetest sound a mother or grandmother ever hears. "Mamu, Mamu," squealed her beloved great-grandbabies as they rushed in to hug her and crawl onto her lap. A long, lanky arm stole around her shoulders for a quick embrace from the firstborn great-grandson. Before she could catch her breath, here came more grandchildren—all of them and their spouses. The clan was complete when Nora's own firstborn and her husband crowded into the pew, and Nora's son made the babies scooch over so he could sit by his mother.

Surely it was God's exquisite timing that caused the young people's chorus and then the entire congregation to stand to their feet and sing out the hymn that says it all: "Come, let us all unite to sing that God is love."

As the beautiful old words rang to the rafters, Nora dried her eyes as she watched her family wrap their arms around each other and lift their voices to heaven.

—VPG

When peace, like a river,
attendeth my way;
When sorrows like sea billows roll;
Whatever my lot,
You have taught me to say,
"It is well, it is well with my soul."
My sin (Oh, the bliss
of this glorious thought!),
My sin—not in part, but the whole—
Is nailed to the cross,
and I bear it no more.
Praise the Lord! Praise the Lord,
O my soul!
And Lord, haste the day my faith shall
be sight:
The clouds will roll back as a scroll,
The trumpet shall sound,
and the Lord shall descend!
Even so, it is well with my soul.

—H. G. Spafford and P. P. Bliss

A Mother's Victory

It was Maysville's first time to make it to the state finals in basketball in twenty-five years. As his team warmed up, Eldon kept glancing toward the entrance to the big fieldhouse. *Where is Mom?* he thought. *Dad promised he'd get her here, even if it took an ambulance.*

Eldon's mother was dying of cancer, but she had let nothing prevent her from attending every basketball game in the past four years. She had even arranged her multiple treatments to fall during times other than basketball season. She was the team's biggest fan, and each player loved her almost as much as his own mother.

Over the past weekend, Eldon's mother had taken a turn for the worse and had been hospitalized. In her determined fashion, she had persuaded the doctors to release her just to attend this championship game, and she promised to check back in immediately afterward. If there was anything she loved more than life itself, it was watching her son play ball, and the prospect of winning state was icing on the cake.

Now Eldon feared something must be wrong. His fears vanished, however, when he saw his teammates run to the gym door and welcome their "team mother." Eldon ran to greet his mom, too. This time his mother wasn't carried to the bleachers. Her wheelchair was rolled to a place of honor at the end of the team's bench, right on the gym floor.

"That's so I can hear you yelling," Eldon told his frail mother, whose eyes still sparkled in anticipation of the event she would get to enjoy. Each boy gave her a quick kiss as he ran out to begin the game. And the game was everything a mother could wish for. Eldon was the high scorer. Her "boys" played flawlessly.

When the final whistle sounded, Maysville had won the state championship, and no one was prouder than Eldon's mother.

When the governor presented the big trophy to the team and its coach, the boys whispered in his ear. The governor nodded and walked over to the smiling lady in the wheelchair.

"Mrs. Green, I'm informed that this trophy belongs to you with a big thanks for your encouragement and support," he said with a formal bow and a big smile. "On behalf of the Maysville team, I proclaim you State Champion Mom!"

The hometowners went wild as they watched their brave friend cry tears of happiness at the honor. And Eldon shed his own private tears as he prayed, "Thank you, God, for honoring my mom."

Eldon's mother died in her sleep that night. She was found lying peacefully, with a smile on her face and a big gold trophy cradled in her arms.

A Love Note from God

In everything
you will have victory,
because this is how I show
my love for you.
Nothing can ever
separate you from me.

—Romans 8:37-39, adapted

Your Love Note to God

Dear God,

_____

_____

_____

_____

_____

_____

_____

I love you. _____

A mother's heart, like primroses,

opens most beautifully

in the evening of life.

—Author Unknown

$\mathcal{B}$ecause you are a mother who
waits on me with trust,
you will become strong again.
You will rise up like an
eagle in the sky.
You will run and not grow weary.
You will walk and not
become tired.

—Isaiah 40:31, adapted

CHAPTER EIGHT

The Vigil

You Are Faithful

Jill stood gazing out her kitchen window as she put her son's lunch in the black metal lunch box he had forgotten that morning. Latching the metal clasps, she smiled at the rioting fall colors of the West Virginia hillsides and relished the splendor of God's creation.

As she filled the glass-lined thermos with hot coffee, Jill heard an explosion. Dynamite blasts were ordinary in coal mining country. And Jill had spent her entire life in and around the mines. Her dad was a mining engineer. Her husband had been a crew chief until he died from the dreaded coal miners' lung disease called "black death." And now her 20-year-old son, Kris, was serving his apprenticeship as a blasting specialist, or "powder monkey" as they were sometimes called.

Kris. Oh, Kris. How desperately she had wanted him to choose some other career. *Get out of the deadly mines. Move away from West Virginia.* But Kris would have none of it. He was bound and determined to follow the family tradition. All her motherly pleadings were useless.

Jill pulled on her old coat to ward off the fall chill, picked up the lunch box and thermos, and pushed open the screen door . . . just as the whistle started to blare.

Doors slamming! Feet running! People yelling! The whistle in a mining town meant only one thing—a cave-in. Jill's throat constricted. Her heart stopped. *Kris!*

Stumbling blindly down the back steps, Jill

began to run toward Mine Number Five. Crying. Tripping. Running. Praying: *God. Oh, God! Please save my Kris.* She dropped the lunch box on the way and arrived at the mine entrance out of breath with most of the tight-knit community.

"George, what about Kris?" she yelled at the foreman.

"Don't know yet, Jill."

"Oh, no!" She shuddered, starting toward the mine.

"Jill, stop!" he commanded. "You know you can't go in there."

"George, this is Kris!" she called over her shoulder as she rushed forward.

More emphatically George yelled, "Jill, if you want to help Kris, stay here!"

She knew George was right. She had been on hand at cave-ins many times through the years. Battling her motherly emotions, she finally stopped just as six men rushed past her into the yawning mouth of the mine with picks, shovels, ropes, and lights. Jill sank down on a fallen log to wait . . . and pray.

The flaming autumn trees somehow didn't seem so brilliant now. They were dulled by the cloud of depression that engulfed Jill and by the tears in her old eyes as she sat by the mine hour after hour. *Eleven men. Buried. Dead or alive? No one knew yet. And Kris.* They were sure now—he was standing beside the powder monkey who had set the blast off that caused the cave-in. They were at the back of the cave, farther in than anyone else.

Rescuers came and went. Relief crews from surrounding mines came in to help. They had been digging for hours. And they came out of the mine exhausted, black with coal dust and sweat, diverting their eyes from Jill and the other families whose sons and husbands and fathers were thought to be in the mine.

About five o'clock rescuers found some of the men who had been working closest to the mine entrance when the blast had occurred. And they brought out six bodies, one at a time, and laid them out side by side on the ground. Slowly going from man to man, Jill trembled as she examined their sooty, tear-stained faces. *No, that's not Kris. No, not him. Not that one. That's not him. No. No. No. Thank you, God. He's not here.* And she numbly returned to her vigil on the log by the mine.

All night long the search went on. Picks picking. Shovels shoveling. Dozens of miners grimly taking turns in the mine. The rest sitting solemnly by the campfire drinking strong, black coffee and trying to rejuvenate themselves for the long hours of backbreaking work they knew were ahead. Carts of loose coal and rock and lumber rumbled out, were dumped, and rumbled back in.

Over and over.

Finally, George walked up and put his hand on Jill's shoulder. "Why don't you go home and get some sleep? We'll come and get you, if we need to."

Simply shaking her head, Jill continued her vigil of waiting and praying, waiting and praying. Some others wandered wearily away to find a solitary place to rest. Young mothers terrified for young fathers took their children home to bed.

Meanwhile, Jill fed the campfire and kept the coffee brewing. She doctored scrapes and cuts of the miners. She held the hands of other mothers and wives and daughters who feared the worst as the night wore wearily on toward dawn.

Three more bodies were brought out. *Not Kris. Not him. No.* "Thank you, God," said Jill aloud as she walked back to her place on the log. *Nine down and two to go,* she thought. *Oh, God, please protect my Kris. He's all I have left now. Please bring him back to me. But even if you don't, Lord, I'll always love you. No matter what, I'll love you.*

The miserable scene continued until dawn the next day. Only a skeleton crew remained. Most everyone had given up hope of finding anyone alive, even George. The odds were just too great. The blast was too strong. The cave-in was too massive. With this realization, most everyone had gone home, sad and worn, to prepare for the grief and funerals they had to face the next day.

But not Jill. She never dozed. Never left. Never gave up hope. She stayed at her mother's post on the log all night. And all the next day. And all the next night. Bone-weary but not beaten, she held up her head bravely to meet the beleaguered eyes of every worker who came out of the mine, hour after depressing hour.

By sunrise of the second day, Jill couldn't feel her hands and feet anymore. They were numb with cold and lack of sleep. So, she got up to walk around. She poured herself yet another cup of the black coffee and rubbed her arms fiercely to increase circulation. She walked around the campfire several times to get her blood pumping again. And she prayed, *Lord, I'm still here. Please bring my Kris out to me safe and sound. I'm not leaving until you do. I trust you.*

Suddenly Jill heard a rumbling, belching sound coming from the mine. With heartsick fear she turned toward the mine entrance just as several miners came running out.

"Get out! Get out! She's going! Run! Everybody run!"

They ran from the mine—ran for their lives. Falling over each other. Hunching down behind huge boulders for protection. Crying with fear. Everyone but Jill. She stood perfectly straight and still in the middle of the clearing facing the mine. Smoke, dust, and debris blew in her face, but somehow she was not afraid. And she stood firmly in place. She was totally at peace.

With a final violent cough, the old mine puffed out a huge billow of charcoal smoke and gas as a mighty rumbling crash of finality came from the belly of the mine. *It's over,* thought Jill. *No one can go back in there now. And no one inside could have survived.* Still, she stood there, waiting.

Jill rubbed her eyes to clean them of the dust. Then, as she focused on the center of the murky cloud, a tall figure came strolling through the foggy smut. And she began to laugh and cry at the same time. It couldn't be! Yes, it was! Out of that choking smoke walked the black, sooty-but-smiling face of her beautiful Kris.

"Hi, Mom," he coughed. "What's for break-fast?" he said, half-joking. "I'm starved."

Jill flung herself into his arms as the other missing miner ran past them to his sobbing wife and little boy. Cheers went up from all the onlookers. Well-wishers crowded around the survivors. And someone joyously pulled the rope that blew the whistle three short blasts—the signal to the village that all was well.

As they walked home arm-in-arm, Jill noticed that the sunrise had set the hillsides ablaze with God's glory—brighter and more splendid than she ever remembered seeing them before. And she thought, *Yes, all is well. Thank you, God. Thank you.*

There was never
a woman like my mother:
She was as gentle as a dove
and as brave as a lioness.

—Andrew Jackson

You're a Miracle

Mom, you're not just a person. You're a miracle! You can turn into anything you need to be in an instant. You're like the star of a science-fiction movie, who drinks a magic potion and transforms into marvelous, superhuman creatures.

You can turn into a nurse, just at the sight of a scrape or scratch. And at the wave of a wand, you appear as Cinderella, ready for the ball.

When trouble threatens, you become a mighty fortress behind which our whole family huddles for protection (even Dad).

Or you wiggle your nose and become a Little

League coach, a Girl Scout leader, a homeroom mother, a Sunday school teacher, a play director, a counselor, a playmate, or a volunteer for Jerry's Kids.

You can be a cook, a maid, a taxi driver, and a referee all in the space of a few minutes. You can turn into a shrewd merchant at a garage sale, an orator at PTA, an enchanting storyteller at the day care center, and a military genius in organizing the neighborhood against crime.

Oh, there's no question about it, Mom. You're not just a person. You're a miracle!

— Mary Hollingsworth

A Love Note
from God

The morning will bring you
word of my unfailing love,
for you have put
your trust in me.

—Psalm 143:8, adapted

Your Love Note to God

Dear God,

_____

_____

_____

_____

_____

_____

_____

_____

I love you. _____

*I*f you have God,
you have a future—
and it's not a dismal one!

—Kay Arthur